Witnessing
Made Simple

Getting
Prepared
to Spread
the Message

William J. Cooper, Jr.

PRESS

ACW Press
Phoenix, Arizona 85013

Witnessing Made Simple
Copyright © 2001 William J. Cooper, Jr.
All rights reserved

Cover design by Alpha Advertising
Interior design by Pine Hill Graphics

Packaged by ACW Press
5501 N. 7th Ave., #502
Phoenix, Arizona 85013
www.acwpress.com
The views expressed or implied in this work do not necessarily reflect those of ACW Press. Ultimate design, content, and editorial accuracy of this work is the responsibility of the author(s).

Publisher's Cataloging-in Publication
(Provided by Quality books, Inc.)

Cooper, William, 1951-
    Witnessing made simple : getting prepared to spread
the message / William J. Cooper, Jr.
    p. cm.
    ISBN 1-892525-46-1

    1. Witness bearing (Christianity)--Handbooks,
manuals, etc.   I. Title

BV4520.C66 2001   269'.2
                                 QBI01-700259

Printed in the United States of America.

Dedication

To Mark, for being an answer to prayer, which provided the opportunity to do this book.

To my sons, Billy and Randy, please forgive me for not being the Christian father I should have been as you were growing up.

To my wife, Paula, you are the cornerstone of our family. You have inspired, encouraged and dedicated your life to making our family strong. I pray this book can serve as an inspiration to you as you continue to grow in the Lord.

To Jeff and Rick for your spiritual guidance and to my brothers and sisters who have provided encouragement along the way.

Contents

     "For God so loved the world that he gave his one and
only Son, that whoever believes in him shall not perish
but have eternal life."

     "for all have sinned and fall short of the glory of God"

     "For the wages of sin is death, but the gift of God is eternal life in Christ Jesus our Lord."

     "But God demonstrates his own love for us in this: While we were still sinners, Christ died for us."

     "If we claim to be without sin, we deceive ourselves and the truth is not in us. If we confess our sins, he is faithful and just and will forgive us our sins and purify us from all unrighteousness."

     "Yet to all who received him, to those who believed in his name, he gave the right to become children of God"

Acknowledgments

Ed Cole, Christian Men's Network, 251 Countryside Court, Southlake, TX 76092. cmn@edcole.org

Promise Keepers, P.O. Box 103001, Denver, CO 80250-3001. www.promisekeepers.com

Northside Fellowship, 6841 Freeman Road, Westerville, Ohio 43082. Pastors, Jeff Dybdahl and Rick Negley.

Introduction

Preparing to Be a
Witness for the Lord

You might ask, "Why a book on witnessing?" The answer is simple; I didn't know how to be a witness for the Lord. As I sit here writing this, I am still not prepared to be a witness. However, by the time I am through writing this, I pray that I will be, and in turn, hope to be able to help others who are going through the same struggle that I am.

So that you may understand, I have not been a student of the Bible. I was involved in Bible studies as a teenager in a youth program but lost my way and haven't studied the Bible for a long time. I am embarrassed to say how long. As I continue to write this book, I have come to realize how much more I could have done in developing my relationship with God. And yet, for all of the lost time, he has always been there, waiting for me.

I received the Lord as my Savior many years ago and I have been ministered to by others, but to actually be a witness myself was and is frightening. All of the standard rationalizations are at work here: fear of rejection, fear that I wouldn't have the conviction, and most significantly, fear that I wouldn't carry the right message because I wasn't sure that I was really equipped with the right ammunition to be a soldier for the Lord.

Of course I was familiar with the old standard, John 3:16:

"For God so loved the world that he gave his one and only Son, that whoever believes in him shall not perish but have eternal life."

We've seen the sign at the football games, held by the man with the crazy hair. And while this may have been enough for him, it wasn't for me. I needed to know more. I needed to be prepared. I needed to have answers to all of the objections that I knew would be forthcoming.

It seemed like a Herculean task and it was too easy to say, *"I'll study on it later."*

A friend asked, "What is witnessing?" For me, witnessing is the sharing of the life I have come to realize through salvation with Jesus Christ. We are all born of sin and through Jesus' sacrifice on the cross and the shedding of his blood for our sins we can realize a life of salvation by receiving him as Lord and Savior in our life. This book will focus on the details of this statement and how it may be used to help others realize a life with Christ.

Getting Prepared

What Do We Need to Do?

Receive the Lord as your Savior.

Don't stop; please keep reading. You see, I just realized as I was writing this—I am trying to learn more about how to witness to other people and this effort, which will be reflected in this book, is also form of witnessing. If you have not yet received the Lord as your Savior, and you finish this book, I will have succeeded in my efforts to be a witness. I will not only have shown you how to be a witness for the Lord, but I will have been a witness for the Lord to you.

You might ask, how did I get started down this path. I attended my second Promise Keepers' meeting in Detroit this year and while the first meeting was inspirational, it wasn't until I attended the second meeting that I felt as if I was being prepared for battle. You see, I am a Vietnam veteran and I know what it is to get prepared for battle. The irony is, when the battle actually starts you often don't feel prepared. It's only after many battles that you start to fall into a pattern or habit. All that you did before becomes second nature, refined by the toils of war.

Why do I bring this up? On the return trip from Detroit I was talking to a friend and was describing my Christian life as a series of battles. It seemed that during my life the times when I drew closer to the Lord, Satan brought a stronger army to oppose me. Each time it seemed like I was beaten back and yet, each time I feel that I have grown stronger. This however, has not prepared me for what I feel is the most important battle—my ability to convey my beliefs to others and be a witness for the Lord.

This was the ultimate battle that I was not prepared for. You see, this meant that I had to approach someone. I would have to invade someone's "personal" space and get close to him or her. It meant that I would have to reach out to them and be a witness and pray with them. As you read this now, do you feel prepared to do this? If so, I applaud you. If not, keep going because there is hope. I know that I most certainly am not prepared. But I hope and pray that I will be by the time I am done with this book.

It is hard enough to say silent prayers by myself let alone pray out loud with others. To be an effective witness meant that I needed to know more of the Scripture than I did. I was a very successful salesperson accustomed to speaking to individuals and large audiences. In spite of this, I was not comfortable or maybe more correctly stated, confident in my abilities to be a witness.

What changed all of this? The last person to present at the Promise Keeper's meeting, Ed Cole, said something that I believe was directed right at me. He simply said, "There are seven verses you need to know to be an effective witness, *only seven.*"

The purpose of this book is to identify those seven verses and to study them and convey to you, the reader, what I have been able to learn from them that will help me to be a witness for the Lord and hopefully, you too.

Realizing that I am in a battle that I cannot win on my own, I have asked for help. Two pastors, Jeff Dybdahl and Rick Negley, have agreed to mentor, guide and otherwise assist me with this effort. For this I give thanks.

You see, before I attended the church that Jeff and Rick serve, I had not stepped into God's temple for almost twenty-five years. I have now been with this wonderful congregation for over three years. This is very important for those reading this who have not been with the Lord for awhile. I keep coming back to the picture we have all seen, entitled "Footprints in the Sand." In my case, he carried me for quite awhile.

Footprints in the Sand

One night I dreamed I was walking along the beach with
    the Lord.
Many scenes from my life flashed across the sky.
In each scene I noticed footprints in the sand.
Sometimes there were two sets of footprints.
Other times there was one set of footprints.
This bothered me because I noticed that during the low
    periods of my life
When I was suffering from anguish, sorrow, or defeat,
I could see only one set of footprints.
So I said to the Lord, "You promised me, Lord,
That if I followed you, you would walk with me always.
But I noticed that during the most trying periods of my
    life
There has only been one set of prints in the sand.
Why, When I have needed you most, you have not been
    there for me?"
The Lord replied,
"The times when you have seen only one set of foot-
    prints
Is when I carried you."

By Mary Stevenson
(Born 11/8/22 Died 1/6/99)

www.foot-print.com, www.wowzone.com/fpnews.htm

I came to realize that I had allowed myself to be influenced by the worldly things that surrounded me. By God's grace, I never lost my belief or convictions and ultimately realized that the Lord was still there waiting for me to return after all that time. All I needed to do was focus my life on him and his Word.

If you have not realized the joys of salvation and the feeling of being close to God, I'm not sure I can relate to you the all of the experiences I have had as a believer in Christ. It is like when I came back from Vietnam; some of what I experienced could be shared with others in a way that they could relate to. However, there are other experiences that I could share that would not be understood unless the person I am relating them to has had a similar experience. The same is true with my Christian life. There are many experiences that I have had that fall into this same set of circumstances. My hope is that I can help you realize a life with Christ and enjoy a richer, fuller relationship with him and be able to share that with others.

The Seven Verses

The Investigation

Overview:

Obviously the first thing I needed to do was find out the seven verses that were behind Mr. Cole's bold claim at the Promise Keepers' meeting.

My first step was to go to the Promise Keepers' web site to get the contact information for Mr. Cole and send him a message asking for the verses he had mentioned. Having completed this task, I waited for him to contact me.

While I waited, not realizing at the time the impact it would have, I loaded an electronic version of the Bible onto my laptop. I had purchased it months ago not realizing that it would be put to this use. Now I anticipated that I would be doing a lot of research and this would make it easy to do so.

Mr. Cole's assistant graciously responded to my inquiry and provided this response.

The Verses:

Rom. 3:23	for all have sinned and fall short of the glory of God
Rom. 6:23	For the wages of sin is death, but the gift of God is eternal life in Christ Jesus our Lord.
Rom. 5:8	But God demonstrates his own love for us in this: While we were still sinners, Christ died for us.
John 3:16	For God so loved the world that he gave his one and only Son, that whoever believes in him shall not perish but have eternal life.
I John 1:8-9	If we claim to be without sin, we deceive ourselves and the truth is not in us. If we confess our sins, he is faithful and just and will forgive us our sins and purify us from all unrighteousness.
John 1:12	Yet to all who received him, to those who believed in his name, he gave the right to become children of God
Rev. 3:20	Here I am! I stand at the door and knock. If anyone hears my voice and opens the door, I will come in and eat with him, and he with me.

Each of the following chapters will focus on one of these verses. I will try to provide:

+ An overview of the book of the Bible that the verse was drawn from;
+ A perspective of the person who wrote the book; and
+ The relevance of the verse to my wanting to be a witness for the Lord.

Guiding Principles:
Setting a foundation for our review

+ The foundation for our belief is based on the Bible.
+ The Bible is God's Word

+ The living Word of God, Jesus, is revealed in the written Word, the Bible
+ Many have tried to disprove the truth of the Bible and have not succeeded.

This raises a very thought-provoking question.

What would our lives be like if the Word, made manifest in Jesus, and recorded in the Bible could not be supported?

Obviously, this has profound implications on someone who wants to be a more effective witness. I just finished reading a small booklet, *More Than A Carpenter* by Josh McDowell, who provides a substantial argument in support of the Word. This was an important event for me because I am not well versed in all of the Scripture that would support my arguments. In Josh's book there are many instances of support by numerous historians, legal experts and other students of the Word who have not been able to dispute the Word of God.

If it were possible for anyone who takes a truly objective view of the Word and its teachings to disprove the Word, then there really wouldn't be a basis for my continuing this effort.

To the contrary, no one that I have heard of has been able to prove the Bible is false. Some have claimed to, but have not been able to prove their claim.

There is a section in Josh's book where he talks about the prophecy of the coming of Jesus. A profound example he uses, from a book written by Peter W. Stoner called *Science Speaks*, addresses the scientific probabilities of fulfilling prophecy, "We find that the chance that any man might have lived down to the present time and fulfilled all eight prophecies is 1 in 10^{17}." Stoner illustrates this by using an example, "We take 10^{17} silver dollars and lay them on the face of Texas. They will cover all of the state two feet deep. Now mark one of these silver dollars and stir the whole mass thoroughly, all over the state. Blindfold a man and tell him that he can travel as far as he wishes, but he must pick up one silver dollar and say that this is the right one. What chance would he have of getting the right one? Just the same chance that the prophets would have had of writing these eight prophecies and having them all come true in any one man, from their day to present time, providing they wrote them in their own wisdom."

As for myself, there have been too many occasions where my prayers have been answered for me not to believe. The foundation for my beliefs, and answers to prayer, started when I was young because of a family situation involving alcohol and abuse and has grown through other trials and tribulations that I have experienced throughout my life. As a child, I would lift up a prayer and believe with peace that my prayers would be answered. I didn't realize it then, but I do now, what it means to surrender the problem to him and the peace that you can realize with total belief that he will answer your prayers. I had forgotten over the years what that felt like.

And yet, as we get older it is harder for us to achieve the same level of peace that we might achieve through total belief as we did when we were younger. We have been raised to believe that modern medicine can deal with most every affliction. Yet people continue to get sick every day. If I were to approach them and say, "Put your TOTAL trust in the Lord and believe with peace that he will provide for your needs," these people would say to me something to the effect, "Yeah right, are you insane, get a life," etc. You see, I have even had these same doubts. As I am writing this I have learned that I have a heart problem. All of the tests have not been completed yet, but there is enough evidence so far that a problem exists. I wrote to a friend in my small group that the human side of me wants to worry over this and yet the spiritual side wants to give it up to the Lord and believe with peace that he will prevail in my life. I am very blessed in that I have known the feeling of total peace before and I continue to receive prayer for my situation. But, you know, Satan really works overtime when he has any opportunity to chip away at your beliefs. Those random thoughts of doubt, anxiety and uncertainty are not from God. It is with faith and trust in God that we can realize peace. It is through his will that we can realize healing and relief from suffering. Many times we can not see the reasoning behind why things happen the way they do but through our trust in him all will be made well.

I do woodworking as a hobby and recently while trimming a piece of shim stock for a new storm door I was hanging, I practically cut the end of my finger off in the table saw through a freak accident. I remember saying at the time that God must have had a reason for me doing something as stupid as this. Can you imagine anyone saying this at a time like this? I must have been nuts, right? Later that night we asked a friend to look at my stupidity as a second opinion to see if I really needed to go to the emergency room; my wife was insisting that I go. The finger was OK, no emergency room, but what happened next was, I believe, part of the plan. You see, my friend was having personal problems, and my wife spent the next two hours talking through the situation with her. My wife had now become part of God's plan in this person's life, brought about in part by my stupidity. We never know how we can or will be used by God to witness to others but if we are not prepared to do so we may never get the chance.

I recently had a job situation where more and more pressure was being placed on me to identify with financial objectives as my source of inspiration. Commissions and financial rewards were the reason for my existence. There wasn't any way I could be considered successful if I couldn't exceed my quota, not just by 10 percent but by 200 percent. I realized that I was being driven in a direction that was not comfortable for me. Yes, the financial rewards were stimulating to me but deep down I knew that something wasn't right. I prayed for deliverance from my bondage to the financial objectives that I was being forced to accept. Within two weeks, while I was making a presentation to a friend, who had taken time off from work to help with a Christian fund-raising effort, I was presented with a job offer that took me out of the situation that I was in. Not only did it remove the feeling of not doing the right thing but I have found that I am surrounded by a fellow group of Christians here at my new place of employment.

I only share these with you so that you will know that prayer is a very strong weapon.

Beth, a dear friend, once said,

> If you want to worry
> Don't pray
> But, If you pray
> Don't worry!

Now, let's take a look at the Bible from a higher elevation to start putting things into perspective.

An Overview of the Old Testament

Law	History	Poetry	Prophecy
Genesis	Joshua	Job	Isaiah
Exodus	Judges	Psalms	Jeremiah
Leviticus	Ruth	Proverbs	Lamentations
Numbers	1 Samuel	Ecclesiastes	Ezekiel
Deuteronomy-	2 Samuel	Song of Songs	Daniel
	1 Kings		Hosea
	2 Kings		Joel
	1 Chronicles		Amos
	2 Chronicles		Obadiah
	Ezra		Jonah
	Nehemiah		Micah
	Esther		Nahum
			Habakkuk
			Zephaniah
			Haggai
			Zechariah
			Malachi
The first five books of the Bible are sometimes called the Law of Moses. They give many of God's laws about how to live.	These twelve historical books cover the occupation of the Promised Land, the time of the Judges, Israel's kings, the fall of the two kingdoms and a return to Jerusalem.	Nearly one third of the Old Testament is written in poetry. These five poetical books ask profound questions about evil, pain, love, wisdom and God.	The seventeen prophetical books account for almost a quarter of the Bible. They are divided into Major Prophets (the first five) and Minor Prophets (the last twelve). The Minor ones are shorter, not less important.

* There are thirty-nine books in the Old Testament library.
* There are four types of writing in the Old Testament: Law, History, Poetry and Prophecy.

An Overview of the New Testament

History	Paul's Letters	Other Letters	Prophecy
Matthew Mark Luke John Acts	Romans 1 Corinthians 2 Corinthians Galatians Ephesians Philippians Colossians 1 Thessalonians 2 Thessalonians 1 Timothy 2 Timothy Titus Philemon	Hebrews James 1 Peter 2 Peter 1 John 2 John 3 John Jude	Revelation
The first four books, called gospels, are not like our modern biographies. But they do give four portraits of Jesus. Acts is part two of Luke, about the early church.	We have thirteen of Paul's letters. Except for one personal one, Philemon, they were all written to groups of Christians.	We don't know who wrote Hebrews. Tradition states that all the writers of the New Testament, except for John, were martyred.	Written by the apostle John, this book has seven letters to churches and numerous visions about God.

* There are twenty-seven books in the New Testament library.
* There are three types of writing in the New Testament: History, Letters and Prophecy.

John 3:16

"For God so loved the world that he gave his one and only Son, that whoever believes in him shall not perish but have eternal life."

Overview:

The Gospel of John stresses the deity of Jesus. It begins with: "In the beginning was the Word, and the Word was with God, and the Word was God [meaning, Jesus was divine]" (John 1:1) and, "And the Word was made flesh, and dwelt among us" (John 1:14).

This was a tough one to start with. In my attempt to understand this passage, I read this to say that in the beginning, prior to the birth of Jesus, there was the Word, God's presence in our mind; and the Word was with God, Jesus resided with God; and the Word was God, Jesus is God. And the Word was made flesh and dwelt among us, Jesus took on human form and walked upon the earth.

An introduction to the book of John:

The complete text surrounding John 3:16 is:

[14]Just as Moses lifted up the snake in the desert, so the Son of Man must be lifted up, [15]that everyone who believes in

him may have eternal life. *¹⁶For God so loved the world that he gave his one and only Son, that whoever believes in him shall not perish but have eternal life. ¹⁷For* God did not send his Son into the world to condemn the world, but to save the world through him. *¹⁸*Whoever believes in him is not condemned, but whoever does not believe stands condemned already because he has not believed in the name of God's one and only Son. [emphasis added]

If we go back to John 3:16, we need some framework for this passage. What is the book of John in relation to the Bible? Fortunately, I am reading a small book called *The Bible Made Easy* which is published by Hendrickson Publishers and it has a number of very good examples that help put everything in context.

You can find the book of John in the New Testament. It is one of a collection of books that are called gospels and present a biography of Jesus from the writer's perspective. The writer was John the Apostle and was one of Jesus' favorites. Jesus entrusted the care of his mother to John at the time of his death.

The book of John is an accounting of Jesus' life as observed by John the Apostle. A simple overview of the book drawn from references in the introduction to the book in the NIV Bible provides this outline:

Outline: The Book of John
  I. Prologue (1:1-18)
 II. Beginnings of Jesus' Ministry (1:19-51)
    A. The Ministry of His forerunner (1:19-34)
    B. Jesus' Introduction to Some Future Disciples (1:35-51)
III. Jesus' Public Ministry: Signs and Discourses (chaps. 2–11)
    A. Changing Water to Wine (2:1-11)
    B. Cleansing the Temple (2:12-25)
    C. Interview with Nicodemus (3:1-21)
    D. Parallel Ministry with John the Baptist (3:22–4:3)

I am using the NIV Study Bible to assist me in writing this book. Many verses in this translation of the Bible are referenced to other verses that can be used to help you understand a little more about what you are reading. Key words or portions of the verse are generally what is referenced. I am including the referenced verses for each of the seven verses as we study.

I have not done this, but as I started putting this chapter together, it would seem that if we started with this one verse and followed its references and then in turn followed all of the references to the new verses, we would eventually read the whole Bible. An interesting theory, for you see, to get the full understanding of the meaning or association with the referenced verses it is important that you read the full passage of verses surrounding the new information. This would obviously lead to reading the whole Bible.

NIV References: John 3:16

"For God so loved the world that he gave his one and only Son, that whoever believes in him shall not perish but have eternal life."

For God so loved
Rom. 5:8   But God demonstrates his own love for us in this: While we were still sinners, Christ died for us.

Eph. 2:4   But because of his great love for us, God, who is rich in mercy,

1 John 4:9,10   This is how God showed his love among us: He sent his one and only Son into the world that we might live through him.
This is love: not that we loved God, but that he loved us and sent his Son as an atoning sacrifice for our sins.

that he gave
Isa. 9:6   For to us a child is born, to us a son is given, and the government will be on his shoulders. And he will be called Wonderful Counselor, Mighty God, Everlasting Father, Prince of Peace.

Rom. 8:32   He who did not spare his own Son, but gave him up for us all—how will he not also, along with him, graciously give us all things?

his one and only Son

Gen. 22:12   "Do not lay a hand on the boy," he said. "Do not do anything to him. Now I know that you fear God, because you have not withheld from me your son, your only son."

John 1:18   No one has ever seen God, but God the One and Only, who is at the Father's side, has made him known.

that whoever believes

John 3:15   that everyone who believes in him may have eternal life.

shall not perish but have eternal life

John 3:36   Whoever believes in the Son has eternal life, but whoever rejects the Son will not see life, for God's wrath remains on him."

John 6:29,40   Jesus answered, "The work of God is this: to believe in the one he has sent."
For my Father's will is that everyone who looks to the Son and believes in him shall have eternal life, and I will raise him up at the last day."

John 11:25,26 Jesus said to her, "I am the resurrection and the life. He who believes in me will live, even though he dies;
and whoever lives and believes in me will never die. Do you believe this?"

Applying what we have learned:

In simple terms, God loves us. But God is a righteous God and judges sin. However, because he loves us, because of our sins, because we were born in sin and need salvation, God sent his one and only son to bear the burden of our sins to the cross on Calvary that we might live through his sacrifice. All we need to do is believe in him and ask to receive him (as in John 1:12).

What have I learned?

+ Jesus was the Son of God.
+ Jesus did not start his ministry until he was about thirty years old.
+ His ministry lasted for about 3 to 3-1/2 years.
+ There were many prophets at this period of time and yet Jesus was the only one who could fulfill the prophecies of the Old Testament.
+ Jesus conducted his ministry in the general area we call Israel today.
+ Jesus conducted his ministry to the Jews, who were the descendants of Abraham and the chosen of God, and the Gentiles alike, who at the time were considered to be the unclean or unworthy, which is one of the reasons the Jews persecuted Jesus.
+ Jesus performed many miracles during his ministry which demonstrates the healing power of faith.
+ Jesus' ministry to the Jews that he was the Son of the Father and that their salvation could only be realized through him was a significant reason for his crucifixion.
+ Jesus was a Jew, but he ministered to the Jews and Gentiles alike.

Romans 3:23

"for all have sinned and fall short of the glory of God"

Overview:

The theme for the whole book of Romans is laid out in 1:16-17:

> [16]I am not ashamed of the gospel, because it is the power of God for the salvation of everyone who believes: first for the Jew, then for the Gentile.
> [17]For in the gospel a righteousness from God is revealed, a righteousness that is by faith from first to last, just as it is written: "The righteous will live by faith."

Righteousness as used throughout this book is summarized in the NIV study notes as: The state of being "in the right" in relation to God.

An introduction to the book of Romans:

The complete text surrounding Romans 3:23 is:

²¹But now a righteousness from God, apart from law, has been made known, to which the Law and the Prophets testify. ²²This righteousness from God comes through faith in Jesus Christ to all who believe. There is no difference, ²³*for all have sinned and fall short of the glory of God,* ²⁴and are justified freely by his grace through the redemption that came by Christ Jesus. ²⁵God presented him as a sacrifice of atonement, through faith in his blood. He did this to demonstrate his justice, because in his forbearance he had left the sins committed beforehand unpunished— ²⁶he did it to demonstrate his justice at the present time, so as to be just and the one who justifies those who have faith in Jesus. [emphasis added]

The book of Romans is a letter the Apostle Paul wrote to the church of Rome preparing for his upcoming visit. It provides a basic system of salvation to the church, which had not received this kind of teaching from an apostle before. A simple overview of the book drawn from references in the introduction to the book in the NIV Bible provides this outline.

Outline: The Book of Romans
    I. Introduction (1:1-15)
    II. Theme: Righteousness from God (1:16-17)
    III. The Unrighteousness of All Mankind (1:18–3:20)
        A. Gentiles (1:18-32)
        B. Jews (2:1–3:8)
        C. Summary: All People (3:9–5:21)
    IV. Righteousness Imputed: Justification (3:21–5:21)
        A. Through Christ (3:21-26)
        B. Received by Faith (3:27–4:25)
            1. The principle established (3:27-31)
            2. The principle illustrated (chap. 4)
        C. The Fruits of Righteousness (5:1-11)

NIV References: Romans 3:23

"for all have sinned and fall short of the glory of God"

for all have sinned

Rom. 3:9   What shall we conclude then? Are we any better?
            Not at all! We have already made the charge that
            Jews and Gentiles alike are all under sin.

The glory that man had before the fall

Gen. 1:26-28   Then God said, "Let us make man in our image, in
               our likeness, and let them rule over the fish of the
               sea and the birds of the air, over the livestock, over
               all the earth, and over all the creatures that move
               along the ground."

So God created man in his own image, in the
image of God he created him; male and female he
created them.
God blessed them and said to them, "Be fruitful
and increase in number; fill the earth and subdue
it. Rule over the fish of the sea and the birds of
the air and over every living creature that moves
on the ground."

Ps. 8:5-6   You made him a little lower than the heavenly
beings and crowned him with glory and honor.
You made him ruler over the works of your hands;
you put everything under his feet:

Eph.4:24   and to put on the new self, created to be like God
in true righteousness and holiness.

Col. 3:10   and have put on the new self, which is being
renewed in knowledge in the image of its Creator.

The believer will again have glory through Christ

Heb. 2:5-9   It is not to angels that he has subjected the world
to come, about which we are speaking.
But there is a place where someone has testified:
"What is man that you are mindful of him, the
son of man that you care for him?
You made him a little lower than the angels; you
crowned him with glory and honor and put everything under his feet." In putting everything under
him, God left nothing that is not subject to him.
Yet at present we do not see everything subject to
him.
But we see Jesus, who was made a little lower than
the angels, now crowned with glory and honor
because he suffered death, so that by the grace of
God he might taste death for everyone.

Applying what we have learned:

What have I learned?

+ No one is righteous, verse 3:10.
+ Through the Law we have become conscious of sin, verse 3:20.
+ Righteousness comes through faith in Jesus Christ.
+ Christ's righteousness (his obedience to God's law and his sacrificial death) will be credited to believers as their own.
+ The Law refers to the moral laws that were provided in the Old Testament which guided the Jews prior to the coming of Christ.

Romans 6:23

"For the wages of sin is death, but the gift of God is eternal life in Christ Jesus our Lord."

Overview:

The whole chapter of Roman 6 is very powerful for the believer and is worth placing a bookmark at. It talks to the position we place ourselves in relative to our confession of faith. This chapter clearly shows the separation of the sinful nature of man and the salvation we receive through Jesus Christ.

An introduction to the book of Romans:

The complete text of Romans 6 is:

¹What shall we say, then? Shall we go on sinning so that grace may increase? ²By no means! We died to sin; how can we live in it any longer? ³Or don't you know that all of us who were baptized into Christ Jesus were baptized into his death?
⁴We were therefore buried with him through baptism into death in order that, just as Christ was raised from the

dead through the glory of the Father, we too may live a new life. [5]If we have been united with him like this in his death, we will certainly also be united with him in his resurrection. [6]For we know that our old self was crucified with him so that the body of sin might be done away with, that we should no longer be slaves to sin— [7]because anyone who has died has been freed from sin.

[8]Now if we died with Christ, we believe that we will also live with him. [9]For we know that since Christ was raised from the dead, he cannot die again; death no longer has mastery over him. [10]The death he died, he died to sin once for all; but the life he lives, he lives to God. [11]In the same way, count yourselves dead to sin but alive to God in Christ Jesus.

[12]Therefore do not let sin reign in your mortal body so that you obey its evil desires. [13]Do not offer the parts of your body to sin, as instruments of wickedness, but rather offer yourselves to God, as those who have been brought from death to life; and offer the parts of your body to him as instruments of righteousness. [14]For sin shall not be your master, because you are not under law, but under grace. [15]What then? Shall we sin because we are not under law but under grace? By no means!

[16]Don't you know that when you offer yourselves to someone to obey him as slaves, you are slaves to the one whom you obey—whether you are slaves to sin, which leads to death, or to obedience, which leads to righteousness? [17]But thanks be to God that, though you used to be slaves to sin, you wholeheartedly obeyed the form of teaching to which you were entrusted. [18]You have been set free from sin and have become slaves to righteousness.

[19]I put this in human terms because you are weak in your natural selves. Just as you used to offer the parts of your body in slavery to impurity and to ever-increasing wickedness, so now offer them in slavery to righteousness leading to holiness. [20]When you were slaves to sin, you were free

from the control of righteousness. [21]What benefit did you reap at that time from the things you are now ashamed of? Those things result in death! [22]But now that you have been set free from sin and have become slaves to God, the benefit you reap leads to holiness, and the result is eternal life. [23]*For the wages of sin is death, but the gift of God is eternal life in Christ Jesus our Lord.*

NIV References: Romans 6:23

"For the wages of sin is death, but the gift of God is eternal life in Christ Jesus our Lord"

For the wages of sin is death

Rom. 6:16   Don't you know that when you offer yourselves to someone to obey him as slaves, you are slaves to the one whom you obey--whether you are slaves to sin, which leads to death, or to obedience, which leads to righteousness?

Rom. 6:21   What benefit did you reap at that time from the things you are now ashamed of? Those things result in death!

Gen. 2:17   but you must not eat from the tree of the knowledge of good and evil, for when you eat of it you will surely die.

Prov. 10:16   The wages of the righteous bring them life, but the income of the wicked brings them punishment.

Ezek. 18:4   For every living soul belongs to me, the father as well as the son--both alike belong to me. The soul who sins is the one who will die.

Rom. 1:32   Although they know God's righteous decree that those who do such things deserve death, they not only continue to do these very things but also approve of those who practice them.

Rom. 5:12   Therefore, just as sin entered the world through one man, and death through sin, and in this way death came to all men, because all sinned.

Rom. 7:5   For when we were controlled by the sinful nature, the sinful passions aroused by the law were at work in our bodies, so that we bore fruit for death.

Rom. 7:13   Did that which is good, then, become death to me? By no means! But in order that sin might be recognized as sin, it produced death in me through what was good, so that through the commandment sin might become utterly sinful.

Rom. 8:6   The mind of sinful man is death, but the mind controlled by the Spirit is life and peace;

Rom. 8:13   For if you live according to the sinful nature, you will die; but if by the Spirit you put to death the misdeeds of the body, you will live,

Gal. 6:7,8   Do not be deceived: God cannot be mocked. A man reaps what he sows.

               The one who sows to please his sinful nature, from that nature will reap destruction; the one who sows to please the Spirit, from the Spirit will reap eternal life.

James 1:15   Then, after desire has conceived, it gives birth to sin; and sin, when it is full grown, gives birth to death.

but the gift of God is eternal life
Matt. 25:46   "Then they will go away to eternal punishment, but the righteous to eternal life."

Applying what we have learned:

We are born of sin and without our belief of Jesus and the salvation it brings, we will continue to live our life in sin. This does not mean that through salvation we will not continue to sin. The battle in our mind, for the control of our mind and the actions we take as a result of our thoughts is a constant day-to-day struggle because Satan will continue to chip away at our new beliefs. I heard on a local Christian radio station a repeat of what I had heard before at a Promise Keepers meeting. The way we can continue to live a Godly life is through prayer. To PRAY is to: Praise God for the many blessings you have received, Repent of the sins you have made, Ask for his help in your daily struggles, and Yield to him that his will might be done.

What have I learned?

- The sacrifice Jesus made on the cross was for our sins.
- We would not have been able to remove ourselves from our sinful nature without this sacrifice.
- Our salvation comes through our belief that Jesus died to save us from our sins.
- Our belief and baptism symbolizes our joining with Jesus.
- Through our faith in Jesus' death and resurrection, we too will live a new life.
- Our salvation through believing Jesus Christ removes us from the sins of our past.
- Our sinful body dies, but our spirit lives with Christ through our acceptance of Him.

Romans 5:8

"But God demonstrates his own love for us in this: While we were still sinners, Christ died for us."

Overview:

While we were still sinners—God didn't discriminate. He didn't pick only the good to save from sin. He chose to sacrifice his son for all of us. Through the sins of one man, Adam, the race of man was condemned and yet through the sacrifice of one man, Jesus, we have the opportunity to be removed from our sins and receive salvation through his sacrifice.

An introduction to the Book of Romans:

The complete text surrounding Romans 5:8 is:

[6]You see, at just the right time, when we were still powerless, Christ died for the ungodly. [7]Very rarely will anyone die for a righteous man, though for a good man someone might possibly dare to die. [8]*But God demonstrates his own love for us in this: While we were still sinners, Christ died for us.* [9]Since we have now been justified by his blood, how much more shall

we be saved from God's wrath through him! [10]For if, when we were God's enemies, we were reconciled to him through the death of his Son, how much more, having been reconciled, shall we be saved through his life! [11]Not only is this so, but we also rejoice in God through our Lord Jesus Christ, through whom we have now received reconciliation.

NIV References: Romans 5:8

"But God demonstrates his own love for us in this: While we were still sinners, Christ died for us."

Christ died for us

John 3:16	"For God so loved the world that he gave his one and only Son, that whoever believes in him shall not perish but have eternal life.
John 15:13	Greater love has no one than this, that he lay down his life for his friends.
1 Pet. 3:18	For Christ died for sins once for all, the righteous for the unrighteous, to bring you to God. He was put to death in the body but made alive by the Spirit,
1 John 3:16	This is how we know what love is: Jesus Christ laid down his life for us. And we ought to lay down our lives for our brothers.
1 John 4:10	This is love: not that we loved God, but that he loved us and sent his Son as an atoning sacrifice for our sins.

Applying what we have learned:

What have I learned?

+ Again, the sacrifice that Jesus makes is for those that accept him.

- Those that choose to reject him will not receive the joy of salvation.
- Our sinful nature would suggest that we would perform a sacrifice for something we want if it has the potential for gain and yet Jesus' sacrifice was for the sinner, who has lost favor with God.
- John 15:13, Greater love has no one than this, that he lay down his life for his friends.
- Jesus laid down his life for us, sinners, so that we might receive forgiveness from the Father for our sins.

1 John 1:8-9

"If we claim to be without sin, we deceive ourselves and the truth is not in us. If we confess our sins, he is faithful and just and will forgive us our sins and purify us from all unrighteousness."

Overview:

A great book for reflection. Full of guidance and truths about ourselves and the life we should lead with Christ.

An introduction to the Book of I John:

The complete text surrounding I John 1:8-9 is:

[5]This is the message we have heard from him and declare to you: God is light; in him there is no darkness at all. [6]If we claim to have fellowship with him yet walk in the darkness, we lie and do not live by the truth. [7]But if we walk in the light, as he is in the light, we have fellowship with one another, and the blood of Jesus, his Son, purifies us from all sin. [8]*If we claim to be without sin, we deceive ourselves and the truth is not in us.* [9]*If we confess our sins, he is faithful and just and will forgive us our sins and purify us from all unrighteousness.* [10]If we claim we have not sinned, we make him out to be a liar and his Word has no place in our lives.

The beginning of chapter 2 is especially relevant to our receiving Christ as our savior.

[1]My dear children, I write this to you so that you will not sin. But if anybody does sin, we have one who speaks to the Father in our defense—Jesus Christ, the Righteous One. [2]He is the atoning sacrifice for our sins, and not only for ours but also for the sins of the whole world.

Outline: The Book of 1 John*

   I. Introduction: The reality of the Incarnation (1:1-4)
  II. The Christian Life as Fellowship with the Father and the Son (1:5-2:28)
     A. Ethical Tests of Fellowship (1:5-2:11)
       1. Moral likeness (1:5-7)
       2. Confession of sin (1:8-2:2)
       3. Obedience (2:3-6)
       4. Love for fellow believers (2:7-11)
     B. Two Digressions (2:12-17)
     C. Christological Test of Fellowship (2:18-28)
       1. Contrast: apostates versus believers (2:18-21)
       2. Person of Christ: the crux of the test (2:22-23)
       3. Persistent belief: key to continuing fellowship (2:24-28)
 III. The Christian Life as Devine Sonship (2:29-4:6)
     A. Ethical Tests of Sonship (2:29-3:24)
       1. Righteousness (2:29-3:10a)
       2. Love (3:10b-24)
     B. Christological Tests of Sonship (4:1-6)
 IV. The Christian Life as a Integration of the Ethical and the Christological (4:7-5:12)
     A. The Ethical Test: Love (4:7-5:5)
       1. The source of love (4:7-16)

---

2. The fruit of love (4:17-19)
3. The relationship of love for God and love for one's spiritual brother (4:20-5:1)
4. Obedience: the evidence of love for God's children (5:2-5)
   B. The Christological Test (5:6-12)
V. Conclusion: Great Christian Certainties (5:13-21)

NIV References: 1 John 8-9

[8]If we claim to be without sin, we deceive ourselves and the truth is not in us. [9]If we confess our sins, he is faithful and just and will forgive us our sins and purify us from all unrighteousness.

If we claim to be without sin

Prov. 20:9   Who can say, "I have kept my heart pure; I am clean and without sin"?

Jer. 2:35   You say, "I am innocent; He is not angry with me." But I will pass judgment on you because you say, "I have not sinned."

Rom. 3:9-19   [9]What shall we conclude then? Are we any better? Not at all! We have already made the charge that Jews and Gentiles alike are all under sin. [10]As it is written: "There is no one righteous, not even one; [11]there is no one who understands, no one who seeks God. [12]All have turned away, they have together become worthless; there is no one who does good, not even one." [13]"Their throats are open graves; their tongues practice deceit." "The poison of vipers is on their lips." [14]"Their mouths are full of cursing and bitterness." [15]"Their feet are swift to shed blood; [16]ruin and misery mark their ways, [17]and the way of peace they do not know." [18]"There is no fear of God before their eyes." [19]Now we know that whatever the law says, it says to those who are under the law, so that every mouth may be silenced and the whole world held accountable to God.

James 3:2   We all stumble in many ways. If anyone is never at fault in what he says, he is a perfect man, able to keep his whole body in check.

we deceive ourselves and the truth is not in us

John 8:44   You belong to your father, the devil, and you want to carry out your father's desire. He was a murderer from the beginning, not holding to the truth, for there is no truth in him. When he lies, he speaks his native language, for he is a liar and the father of lies.

1 John 2:4   The man who says, "I know him," but does not do what he commands is a liar, and the truth is not in him.

If we confess our sins, he is faithful and just and will forgive us our sins

Ps. 32:5   Then I acknowledged my sin to you and did not cover up my iniquity. I said, "I will confess my transgressions to the LORD"— and you forgave the guilt of my sin. Selah.

Ps. 51:2   Wash away all my iniquity and cleanse me from my sin.

Prov. 28:13   He who conceals his sins does not prosper, but whoever confesses and renounces them finds mercy.

and purify us from all unrighteousness

1 John 1:7   But if we walk in the light, as he is in the light, we have fellowship with one another, and the blood of Jesus, his Son, purifies us from all sin.

Applying what we have learned:

What have I learned?

+ We must confess of our sins.
+ A person cannot believe that they are without sin and live a life with Christ.
+ We must give up our sins to the one who sacrificed himself for us to his father so that we might live.

John 1:12

"Yet to all who received him, to those who believed in his name, he gave the right to become children of God"

Overview:
The beginning of Jesus' ministry is defined in chapter 1 of the book of John. This is where John the Baptist identifies Jesus as the Messiah.

John 1:32-34   Then John gave this testimony: "I saw the Spirit  come down from heaven as a dove and remain on him. I would not have known him, except that the one who sent me to baptize with water told me, 'The man on whom you see the Spirit come down and remain is he who will baptize with the Holy Spirit. I have seen and I testify that this is the Son of God.'"

An introduction to the book of John:

The complete text surrounding John 1:12 is:

⁶There came a man who was sent from God; his name was John. ⁷He came as a witness to testify concerning that light, so that through him all men might believe. ⁸He himself was not the light; he came only as a witness to the light. ⁹The true light that gives light to every man was coming into the world. ¹⁰He was in the world, and though the world was made through him, the world did not recognize him. ¹¹He came to that which was his own, but his own did not receive him. ¹²*Yet to all who received him, to those who believed in his name, he gave the right to become children of God—* ¹³children born not of natural descent, nor of human decision or a husband's will, but born of God. ¹⁴The Word became flesh and made his dwelling among us. We have seen his glory, the glory of the One and Only, who came from the Father, full of grace and truth.

Outline

For the outline to the book of John see the chapter on John 3:16.

NIV References: John 1:12

"Yet to all who received him, to those who believed in his name, he gave the right to become children of God."

to those who believed

John 1:7   He came as a witness to testify concerning that light, so that through him all men might believe.

John 3:15   that everyone who believes in him may have eternal life.

in his name

1 John 3:23   And this is his command: to believe in the name
              of his Son, Jesus Christ, and to love one another
              as he commanded us.

he gave the right to become children of God

Deut. 14:1   You are the children of the LORD your God. Do
              not cut yourselves or shave the front of your heads
              for the dead, for you are a people holy to the
              LORD your God. Out of all the peoples on the
              face of the earth, the LORD has chosen you to be
              his treasured possession.

Rom. 8:14   because those who are led by the Spirit of God are
              sons of God.

Rom. 8:16   The Spirit himself testifies with our spirit that we
              are God's children.

Rom. 8:21   that the creation itself will be liberated from its
              bondage to decay and brought into the glorious
              freedom of the children of God.

Eph. 5:1   Be imitators of God, therefore, as dearly loved
              children.

1 John 3:1,2 How great is the love the Father has lavished on
              us, that we should be called children of God! And
              that is what we are! The reason the world does not
              know us is that it did not know him. Dear friends,
              now we are children of God, and what we will be
              has not yet been made known. But we know that
              when he appears, we shall be like him, for we shall
              see him as he is.

Applying what we have learned:

What have I learned?

- We must "receive" the gift of God's grace to become members of his family.
- It is not because of actions on our own part that we will realize salvation.

Eph. 2:8,9   For it is by grace you have been saved, through faith—and this not from yourselves, it is the gift of God— not by works, so that no one can boast.

John 1:13   children born not of natural descent, nor of human decision or a husband's will, but born of God.

Revelation 3:20

"Here I am! I stand at the door and knock. If anyone hears my voice and opens the door, I will come in and eat with him, and he with me."

Overview:

Revelation is the closing book and the only book in the New Testament written in a prophetic style. The word "revelation" means to "take the cover off." This book is about the uncovering of the glory of Christ and the future we will have with him as believers. There are four general interpretations of Revelation: the events have already taken place, a panoramic view of the first century to the coming of Christ, the triumph of good over evil and a prophecy of the second coming of Christ.

An introduction to the Book of Revelation:

The complete text surrounding Revelation 3:20 is:

[14]"To the angel of the church in Laodicea write: These are the Words of the Amen, the faithful and true witness, the ruler of God's creation. [15]I know your deeds, that you are neither cold nor hot. I wish you were either one or the

other! ¹⁶So, because you are lukewarm—neither hot nor cold—I am about to spit you out of my mouth. ¹⁷You say, 'I am rich; I have acquired wealth and do not need a thing.' But you do not realize that you are wretched, pitiful, poor, blind and naked. ¹⁸I counsel you to buy from me gold refined in the fire, so you can become rich; and white clothes to wear, so you can cover your shameful nakedness; and salve to put on your eyes, so you can see. ¹⁹Those whom I love I rebuke and discipline. So be earnest, and repent. ²⁰*Here I am! I stand at the door and knock. If anyone hears my voice and opens the door, I will come in and eat with him, and he with me.* ²¹To him who overcomes, I will give the right to sit with me on my throne, just as I overcame and sat down with my Father on his throne. ²²He who has an ear, let him hear what the Spirit says to the churches."

Make a commitment. Salvation cannot come through indifference or lack of commitment. A decision must be made. Good works are not a guarantee of salvation. You must believe in the sacrifice that Jesus made for our sins. We are often led to believe that if we are a good person, do good works, maintain a Christian-like lifestyle, etc., we will go to heaven. This is not true. Unless you believe on the one sent from God who was sacrificed for our sins and raised from the dead, you will not see the kingdom of God.

Outline: The Book of Revelation*

    I. Introduction (1:1-8)
        A. Prologue (1:1-3)
        B. Greetings and Doxology (1:4-8)
    II. Jesus among the Seven Churches (1:9-20)
   III. The Letters to the Seven Churches (chaps. 2-3)
        A. Ephesus (2:1-7)
        B. Smyrna (2:8-11)

C. Pergamum (2:12-17)
D. Thyatira (2:18-29)
E. Sardis (3:1-6)
F. Philadelphia (3:7-13)
G. Laodicea (3:14-22)
IV. The Throne, the Scroll and the Lamb (chaps. 4-5)
A. The Throne in Heaven (chap. 4)
B. The Seven-Sealed Scroll (5:1-5)
C. The Lamb Slain (5:6-14)
V. The Seven Seals (6:1–8:1)
A. First Seal: The White Horse (6:1-2)
B. Second Seal: The Red Horse (6:3-4)
C. Third Seal: The Black Horse (6:5-6)
D. Fourth Seal: The Pale Horse (6:7-8)
E. Fifth Seal: The Souls under the Altar (6:9-11)
F. Sixth Seal: The Great Earthquake (6:12-17)
G. The Sealing of the 144,000 (7:1-8)
H. The Great Multitude (7:9-17)
I. Seventh Seal: Silence in Heaven (8:1)
VI. The Seven Trumpets (8:2–11:19)
A. Introduction (8:2-5)
B. First Trumpet: Hail and Fire Mixed with Blood (8:6-7)
C. Second Trumpet: A Mountain Thrown into the Sea (8:8-9)
D. Third Trumpet: The Star Wormwood (8:10-11)
E. Fourth Trumpet: A Third of the Sun, Moon and Stars Struck (8:12-13)
F. Fifth Trumpet: The Plague of Locusts (9:1-12)
G. Sixth Trumpet: Release of the Four Angels (9:13-21)
H. The Two Witnesses (11:1-14)
I. Seventh Trumpet: Judgements and Rewards (11:15-19)
VII. Various Personages and Events (chaps. 12-14)
A. The Woman and the Dragon (chap. 12)
B. The Two Beasts (chap. 13)
C. The Lamb and the 144,000 (14:1-5)

In John's letter to Laodicea he instructs them to lay down the false confidence they have born of material possessions and put on the clothes of salvation. Verse 19, "Those whom I love I rebuke and discipline. So be earnest, and repent." If we care for someone and we know that they have done wrong we rebuke them—not out of hate or spite but out of love. So too is God's love for us.

NIV References: Revelation 3:20

"Here I am! I stand at the door and knock. If anyone hears my voice and opens the door, I will come in and eat with him, and he with me."

Here I am! I stand at the door

Matt. 24:33   Even so, when you see all these things, you know that it is near, right at the door.

James 5:9   Don't grumble against each other, brothers, or you will be judged. The Judge is standing at the door!

Luke 12:36   like men waiting for their master to return from a wedding banquet, so that when he comes and knocks they can immediately open the door for him.

I will come in

Rom. 8:10   But if Christ is in you, your body is dead because of sin, yet your spirit is alive because of righteousness.

Applying what we have learned:

What have I learned?
+ Do not deceive yourself; material possessions will not guarantee salvation.
+ To cover ourselves and to protect ourselves from the power of the darkness we must clothe ourselves with the word of God.
+ Jesus will return, at a time when we least expect him, and we must be ready.

Receiving Christ

Assurance of Salvation

A Simple Prayer

Wayne, a dear friend, presented me with a gift from the Gideons, a New Testament Bible that I could use for daily reference. I took it to work and put it into the drawer of my desk and didn't look at it. This morning, while I was doing some research I came across this Bible and I realized, thank you Lord for continuing to open my eyes and thoughts to you, that I should be carrying it around with me. In the back of this Bible is a section on witnessing, a simple prayer for salvation and Scriptures for assurance of that salvation. The simple prayer in the back of this Bible is relevant to add at this point—a simple prayer asking God to come into your life.

> Confessing to God that I am a sinner, and believing that the Lord Jesus Christ died for my sins on the cross and was raised for my justification, I do now receive and confess him as my personal Savior.

Name: _____

Date: _____

If you would like to receive Jesus as your Lord and Savior all you have to do is ask him by reciting this prayer. If you do, I ask that you make a copy of this page and send it to Northside Fellowship as a symbol of your receiving Christ in your life. The address is in the acknowledgement section. Also, indicate if you need a Bible and we will be glad to send you one.

What assurances do I have of my salvation?

Rom. 10:9 That if you confess with your mouth, "Jesus is Lord," and believe in your heart that God raised him from the dead, you will be saved.

John 5:24 "I tell you the truth, whoever hears my Word and believes him who sent me has eternal life and will not be condemned; he has crossed over from death to life."

I John 5:13 I write these things to you who believe in the name of the Son of God so that you may know that you have eternal life.

John 20:31 But these are written that you may believe that Jesus is the Christ, the Son of God, and that by believing you may have life in his name.

Living a Life with Christ

Guidelines for Strengthening Your Relationship

I am providing in this section what I call a recipe for spiritual success. What do I mean by success? It is the ability to live a spiritual life and enjoy success in your battle with darkness. You too have had many battles with Satan and will continue to. What I have come to realize through this effort is that the suit of armor I needed to be able to sustain the good fight was there all the time and all I had to do was put it on.

Daily Prayer

The first ingredient or piece of armor is prayer. This is a really difficult one. It was for me and I know it is for you. I said my prayers when I was young like most everyone else, "Now I lay me down to sleep...," and it was easy; it was night time, no one around to see or hear me. I didn't have to expose myself or my insecurities to someone else. As I grew older, this became even more difficult. The circumstance that changed all of that was joining a small group fellowship. While everyone was encouraged to pray in this group, it wasn't required. But, what they prayed for stirred my heart and I realized that I was in a situation where no one would ridicule or demean me for what I said and that they were actually support-ive and encouraging. I felt a peace that I had not felt before. It is still hard to pray with others, but it is getting easier. Like everything else, the more you practice the easier it gets.

I now begin each day by praying this prayer,

"Lord, I give thanks for the blessings you have bestowed on my family and me. I pray that you open our eyes, ears, mind and heart that we might be able to see, hear, know and feel your presence in our life today so that we may be an effective witness for you to others. Lord please help me to be a witness to one person today. In Jesus name, Amen."

It took a long time for me to be able to do this. You see, God is all around us. All we need to do is open ourselves to him and he will reveal himself to us.

Bible Study

The second ingredient or piece of armor you need is an under-standing of the Scripture in the Bible. As I stated earlier, the foun-dation for our beliefs is the Word of God, which is captured in the Bible. This is another important activity, daily study of the Bible.

You may not have realized it but I have made a very bold state-ment here. You see I did not say read the Bible, I said study the Bible. The difference for me was in understanding all of those ref-erence things that were stuck in the middle of the page. It was read-ing the introduction which explained how to understand what those funny symbols meant and how to use them. It was learning the abbreviation or where to look for the abbreviations. It was in learning about the ancient texts relating to the Old Testament It was learning about the units of measure and the subject index and the notes index and last but not least the Concordance.

It was in taking a single verse and following all of the references to be able to draw conclusions for myself and then testing those conclusions with others in small group or individual discussion.

Fellowship (koinonia)

The third ingredient or piece of armor that we desperately need is fellowship or what is often referred to by the term *koinonia*.

I am blessed in that my pastor, Jeff Dybdahl, led our small group on the subject of Koinonia and I will include reference here to the passages he supplied as a reference for our discussion that night.

What is *koinonia* (fellowship)—

Acts 2:42-47   [42]They devoted themselves to the apostles' teaching and to the fellowship, to the breaking of bread and to prayer.
[43]Everyone was filled with awe, and many wonders and miraculous signs were done by the apostles.
[44]All the believers were together and had everything in common.
[45]Selling their possessions and goods, they gave to anyone as he had need.
[46]Every day they continued to meet together in the temple courts. They broke bread in their homes and ate together with glad and sincere hearts,
[47]praising God and enjoying the favor of all the people. And the Lord added to their number daily those who were being saved.

John 13:35   By this all men will know that you are my disciples, if you love one another."

I Cor. 12:12-14 [12]The body is a unit, though it is made up of many parts; and though all its parts are many, they form one body. So it is with Christ.
[13]For we were all baptized by one Spirit into one body—whether Jews or Greeks, slave or free—and

we were all given the one Spirit to drink. ¹⁴Now the body is not made up of one part but of many.

I Cor. 12:26   If one part suffers, every part suffers with it; if one part is honored, every part rejoices with it.

Heb. 10:25   Let us not give up meeting together, as some are in the habit of doing, but let us encourage one another—and all the more as you see the Day approaching.

II Cor. 6:14   Do not be yoked together with unbelievers. For what do righteousness and wickedness have in common? Or what fellowship can light have with darkness?

I John 1:3   We proclaim to you what we have seen and heard, so that you also may have fellowship with us. And our fellowship is with the Father and with his Son, Jesus Christ.

Rom. 15:26   For Macedonia and Achaia were pleased to make a contribution for the poor among the saints in Jerusalem.

II Cor. 8:24   Therefore show these men the proof of your love and the reason for our pride in you, so that the churches can see it.

Phil. 1:3-5   ³I thank my God every time I remember you.
⁴In all my prayers for all of you, I always pray with joy
⁵because of your partnership in the gospel from the first day until now.

Eph. 2:19   Consequently, you are no longer foreigners and aliens, but fellow citizens with God's people and members of God's household.

II Cor. 13:14   May the grace of the Lord Jesus Christ, and the love of God, and the fellowship of the Holy Spirit be with you all.

Phil. 2:1   If you have any encouragement from being united with Christ, if any comfort from his love, if any fellowship with the Spirit, if any tenderness and compassion

I Cor. 1:9   God, who has called you into fellowship with his Son Jesus Christ our Lord, is faithful.

I Cor. 10:16   Is not the cup of thanksgiving for which we give thanks a participation in the blood of Christ? And is not the bread that we break a participation in the body of Christ?

Phil. 3:10   I want to know Christ and the power of his resurrection and the fellowship of sharing in his sufferings, becoming like him in his death.

Fellowship with others, especially in our small groups, has provided a richly rewarding experience for me. It is difficult now to think of how I could have grown without this influence on my life. In the daily battles that we wage in trying to maintain control of our mind and not let Satan influence our beliefs and actions, it is critically important that we have others we can have fellowship with, to discuss our trials and tribulations, who can help us keep our focus.

Witness

The next ingredient or piece of armor is witnessing. Witnessing to others is the basis for this book. While I have grown in my ability to pray and I am spending more time in reading and researching the Bible, and my fellowship with others in small groups been rewarding, I am just now, after all this, starting to open up to others. To my amazement, this book has been a magnet to others and I am getting to know people around me at work and elsewhere, that I would not have come to know. We all have trouble approaching others and yet I have found that people want to share in this effort. They too want to be an effective witness. While I suspected that there would be others like me, it is encouraging to realize the support I have received through prayer and kind words for this effort.

I hope it has been a benefit to you. It has helped equip me with a suit of armor to wear in my day-to-day struggles with the darkness of Satan and his efforts to invade our mind with unclean thoughts that affect our ability to be effective witnesses for the Lord.

Our salvation does not guarantee us a clean, sinless life. To the contrary, in my life it has meant that Satan has redoubled his efforts to influence my thoughts and actions. And yet, as I stated previously, I have managed to overcome these setbacks and rise a stronger person in the Lord. Had I been applying this recipe and equipped myself with this suit of armor, my trials and tribulations, I believe, would not have been as great as they have been. The only value I can say that I have realized is potentially a more powerful witness because of the struggles I have gone through and my ability to share those with others who are now going through the same trials.

I present this challenge to you. During a Christian broadcast on the local radio station I heard something that was very disconcerting to me. How many of you can identify with this phrase, "two all beef patties, special sauce...." Yes we all probably know not only this phrase but countless others. And yet, how many of you without looking back, can recite the seven verses I have presented to you in this book. To be a witness is to know that which you are witnessing about. I have accepted this challenge for myself, to not only know the seven verses and their meaning but also the names and significance of each book of the Bible. This will become my breastplate in my suit of armor, the part that protects my heart so that it may become more pure in the eyes of the Lord.

Sometimes a crutch helps us walk; I have a terrible memory and I did this to help me remember.

ALL	For ALL have sinned and fall short of the glory of God. (No one is excluded.)
WAGES	For the WAGES of sin is death, but the gift of God is eternal life in Christ Jesus our Lord. (Our sinful wages earn us death, through Jesus we have eternal life.)
DEMONSTRATES	But God DEMONSTRATES his own love for us in this: While we were still sinners, Christ died for us. (Christ died for us as a demonstration of God's love for us, in spite of the fact that we were sinners.)
WORLD	For God so loved the WORLD that he gave his one and only Son, that whoever believes in him shall not perish but have eternal life. (Could you, would you sacrifice your ONLY son to save others from sin?)
DECEIVE	If we claim to be without sin, we DECEIVE ourselves and the truth is not in us. If we confess our sins, he is faithful and just and will forgive us our sins and purify us from all unrighteousness. (We are fools to think we can do this without him.)
RECEIVE	Yet to all who RECEIVED him, to those who believed in his name, he gave the right to become children of God. (He is there, all we have to do is receive him into our life.)
KNOCK	Here I am! I stand at the door and KNOCK. If anyone hears my voice and opens the door, I will come in and eat with him, and he with me. (Reach out to him and he will come in; all you need to do is ask.)

It is worth adding at this point—I have completed the necessary tests to determine the reason for the chest pains and heart condition. I had a heart cath procedure done and unbeknownst to me the doctor had already scheduled a balloon procedure. Obviously, he was confident that there was a blockage or something that warranted that procedure. I had received many prayers for God's intervention in my situation asking that whatever was wrong that the Lord apply his healing hand and guide the doctors in their efforts. A very dear brother in Christ said a prayer for me at the hospital asking that whatever was wrong, that God apply his healing hand so that the problem could be corrected, if that be his will. I went into surgery with a feeling of peace that the Lord had already done what we had asked of him. The outcome was much different than we expected. There was no blockage, at all. A virus had attacked my heart muscle and weakened it, which caused my blood pressure to rise higher than normal during periods of physical exertion. However, there is a possibility that it can be healed. I praise God for his intervention and for the many prayers I received. I truly believe that without this the outcome would have been more severe.

What's Next?

How Do I Apply
What I Have Learned?

Networking

It has been said that if everyone contacted only two other people, in a very short period of time the entire population of the world will have been networked together. Think of the possibilities.

Instead, if what I have presented to you here in this book compels you to do so, simply pass a copy on to two other people as you become a witness to them.

Just think of what could be accomplished if we all could reach out to only two other people in need and be able to help them realize a life with Christ.

I think of a stone being cast out into a pond and the ripples that extend far beyond the initial contact. We will never know what profound impact we will have on others and this world through our witnessing, but an example might help.

The Ripple Effect

Recent surveys of pastors reveal that a startling percentage of them are not convinced they are having any real impact on *anyone*. This is particularly regrettable because *making a difference* is the very reason most pastors go into the ministry.

A Sunday school teacher named Edward Kimball wasn't always sure his life had much consequence, either. In 1858, he at least was able to lead a shoe clerk to Christ. The clerk, Dwight L. Moody, became an evangelist, and in 1879 Moody awakened an evangelistic zeal in the heart of F. B. Meyer, the pastor of a small church in New England. Meyer, preaching on a college campus, won a student named J. Wilbur Chapman to Christ.

While Chapman was engaged in YMCA work, he employed a former baseball player named Billy Sunday to help with evangelistic meetings. Sunday held a series of services in the Charlotte, North Carolina area, and a group of local men were so enthused by the meetings that they planned another campaign. This time they brought preacher Mordecai F. Ham to town.

During one of his meetings, a young man named Billy Graham yielded his life to Christ. Since then, millions have heard the gospel through Graham's ministry. *Kimball had started quite a ripple effect!* So can you.

In fact, you're probably already making a greater impact than you think.

—Jim Buchan

You may never know the full effect your being a witness will have on others. But trust in the Lord that it will reach the right person. Even though you may be unsuccessful in reaching someone, you may have opened their mind and their heart to receiving him through additional witnessing by others.

Conclusion

Principles for Witnessing

Genesis 1:1—"In the beginning God created the heavens and the earth."

I heard a recent Christian radio broadcast that was focused on the great debate. It is this simple—if we do not believe in this one statement, there is no basis for the Christian faith. To be an effective witness we must first have the belief and conviction that this is the foundation for our belief.

Therefore, the Bible is the guiding principle for how we should live our lives as Christians.

The Old Testament provided the Laws, which we chose to ignore and subsequently brought the wrath of God upon us which, aside from the faith of a few good men, would have ended our existence. The "Covenant" God reached with Abraham in Genesis provided the promise of a Messiah or one who would deliver us from the bondage of sin.

God has demonstrated his love for man and yet on many occasions has brought his wrath down upon us because of our sinful nature. Realizing that we are sinful and because of his love for us, God sent his one and only son to us as a sacrifice that we might realize the joy of the kingdom of Christ through our salvation based on our belief that he died for our sins. Out of our baptism we are raised anew in Christ and the past is washed away. As the spirit descended upon Christ at the time of his baptism, so too will we realize the spirit of salvation through our belief in the sacrifice God has made through his son Jesus Christ.

Accept the Lord as your savior and be a witness for him.

John 15

[1]"I am the true vine, and my Father is the gardener. [2]He cuts off every branch in me that bears no fruit, while every branch that does bear fruit he prunes so that it will be even more fruitful. [3]You are already clean because of the word I have spoken to you. [4]Remain in me, and I will remain in you. No branch can bear fruit by itself; it must remain in the vine. Neither can you bear fruit unless you remain in me.

[5]"I am the vine; you are the branches. If a man remains in me and I in him, he will bear much fruit; apart from me you can do nothing. [6]If anyone does not remain in me, he is like a branch that is thrown away and withers; such branches are picked up, thrown into the fire and burned. [7]If you remain in me and my words remain in you, ask whatever you wish, and it will be given you. [8]This is to my Father's glory, that you bear much fruit, showing your-selves to be my disciples. [9]"As the Father has loved me, so have I loved you. Now remain in my love. [10]If you obey my commands, you will remain in my love, just as I have obeyed my Father's commands and remain in his love. [11]I have told you this so that my joy may be in you and that your joy may be complete. [12]My command is this: Love each other as I have loved you. [13]Greater love has no one

than this, that he lay down his life for his friends. [14]You are my friends if you do what I command. [15]I no longer call you servants, because a servant does not know his master's business. Instead, I have called you friends, for everything that I learned from my Father I have made known to you. [16]You did not choose me, but I chose you and appointed you to go and bear fruit—fruit that will last. Then the Father will give you whatever you ask in my name. [17]This is my command: Love each other.

[18]"If the world hates you, keep in mind that it hated me first. [19]If you belonged to the world, it would love you as its own. As it is, you do not belong to the world, but I have chosen you out of the world. That is why the world hates you. [20]Remember the words I spoke to you: 'No servant is greater than his master.' If they persecuted me, they will persecute you also. If they obeyed my teaching, they will obey yours also. [21]They will treat you this way because of my name, for they do not know the One who sent me. [22]If I had not come and spoken to them, they would not be guilty of sin. Now, however, they have no excuse for their sin. [23]He who hates me hates my Father as well. [24]If I had not done among them what no one else did, they would not be guilty of sin. But now they have seen these miracles, and yet they have hated both me and my Father. [25]But this is to fulfill what is written in their Law: 'They hated me without reason.'

[26]"When the Counselor comes, whom I will send to you from the Father, the Spirit of truth who goes out from the Father, he will testify about me. [27]And you also must testify, for you have been with me from the beginning.

God, bless this reader that they may take these words to heart and become disciples and bear witness to your glory. Amen.

Epilogue

If you have found value in what I have provided to you I would like to ask a favor. Our church is reaching out to the youth of our generation and I strongly believe that the battle lines have been drawn. We desperately need to create a ministry to the youth of our world. The best way to do this is to have our youth reach out to others through a Christian Ministry.

ALL of the proceeds of this book will be used to help build a Youth Center and create an Internet site developed by the young Christians of our community, which will be youth focused and will help to carry this message around the world. I am asking for your prayers that this effort succeed. If you would like to help with this effort, I would ask that you please forward a donation to:

Northside Fellowship
WFD - Youth Ministry
6841 Freeman Road
Westerville, Ohio 43082 USA

Thank you and may God bless you.

Appendix

Comparisons with Other Translations of the Bible

Salvation

John 3:16

— King James John 3:16

> For God so loved the world, that he gave his only begotten Son, that whosoever believeth in him should not perish, but have everlasting life.

— American Standard John 3:16

> For God so loved the world, that he gave his only begotten Son, that whosoever believeth on him should not perish, but have eternal life.

— New International John 3:16

> "For God so loved the world that he gave his one and only Son, that whoever believes in him shall not perish but have eternal life.

— Revised Standard John 3:16

> For God so loved the world that he gave his only Son, that whoever believes in him should not perish but have eternal life.

— **Simple English John 3:16**

> God loved the people of the world so much that He gave up His only Son. Every person who commits himself to Jesus will not be destroyed. Instead, that person will have eternal life.

Romans 3:23

— **King James Romans 3:23**

> For all have sinned, and come short of the glory of God;

— **American Standard Romans 3:23**

> for all have sinned, and fall short of the glory of God;

— **New International Romans 3:23**

> for all have sinned and fall short of the glory of God,

— **Revised Standard Romans 3:23**

> since all have sinned and fall short of the glory of God,

— **Simple English Romans 3:23**

> because everyone has sinned and is far away from God's glory.

Romans 6:23

— **King James Romans 6:23**

> For the wages of sin is death; but the gift of God is eternal life through Jesus Christ our Lord.

— **American Standard Romans 6:23**

> For the wages of sin is death; but the free gift of God is eternal life in Christ Jesus our Lord.

— **New International Romans 6:23**

> For the wages of sin is death, but the gift of God is eternal life in Christ Jesus our Lord.

— **Revised Standard Romans 6:23**

> For the wages of sin is death, but the free gift of God is eternal life in Christ Jesus our Lord.

— **Simple English Romans 6:23**

> The pay for sinning is death, but God's gift is eternal life in Christ Jesus, our Lord.

Romans 5:8

— King James Romans 5:8

But God commendeth his love toward us, in that, while we were yet sinners, Christ died for us.

— American Standard Romans 5:8

But God commendeth his own love toward us, in that, while we were yet sinners, Christ died for us.

— New International Romans 5:8

But God demonstrates his own love for us in this: While we were still sinners, Christ died for us.

— Revised Standard Romans 5:8

But God shows his love for us in that while we were yet sinners Christ died for us.

— Simple English Romans 5:8

But God reassures us of His love for us in this way: While we were still sinners, Christ died for us!

I John 1:8-9

— King James 1 John 1:8-9

If we say that we have no sin, we deceive ourselves, and the truth is not in us.

If we confess our sins, he is faithful and just to forgive us our sins, and to cleanse us from all unrighteousness.

— American Standard 1 John 1:8-9

If we say that we have no sin, we deceive ourselves, and the truth is not in us.

If we confess our sins, he is faithful and righteous to forgive us our sins, and to cleanse us from all unrighteousness.

— New International 1 John 1:8-9

If we claim to be without sin, we deceive ourselves and the truth is not in us.

If we confess our sins, he is faithful and just and will forgive us our sins and purify us from all unrighteousness.

— Revised Standard 1 John 1:8-9

> If we say we have no sin, we deceive ourselves, and the truth is not in us.

> If we confess our sins, he is faithful and just, and will forgive our sins and cleanse us from all unrighteousness.

— Simple English 1 John 1:8-9

> If we say, "We have no sin!" then we are only fooling ourselves. The truth is not in us.

> However, if we admit our sins, then God will forgive us. We can trust God; He does what is right. He will cleanse us from every evil thing.

John 1:12

— King James John 1:12

> But as many as received him, to them gave he power to become the sons of God, even to them that believe on his name:

— American Standard John 1:12

> But as many as received him, to them gave he the right to become children of God, even to them that believe on his name:

— New International John 1:12

> Yet to all who received him, to those who believed in his name, he gave the right to become children of God—

— Revised Standard John 1:12

> But to all who received him, who believed in his name, he gave power to become children of God;

— Simple English John 1:12

> But he gave the right to become God's children to those who did accept him, to those who believe in his name.

Revelation 3:20

— King James Revelation 3:20

> Behold, I stand at the door, and knock: if any man hear my voice, and open the door, I will come in to him, and will sup with him, and he with me.

— **American Standard Revelation 3:20**

> Behold, I stand at the door and knock: if any man hear my voice and open the door, I will come in to him, and will sup with him, and he with me.

— **New International Revelation 3:20**

> Here I am! I stand at the door and knock. If anyone hears my voice and opens the door, I will come in and eat with him, and he with me.

— **Revised Standard Revelation 3:20**

> Behold, I stand at the door and knock; if any one hears my voice and opens the door, I will come in to him and eat with him, and he with me.

— **Simple English Revelation 3:20**

> Listen, I stand at the door. I am knocking. If anyone hears my voice and opens the door, I will come inside with him. We will have dinner together.

Assurance

Romans 10:9

— **King James Romans 10:9**

> That if thou shalt confess with thy mouth the Lord Jesus, and shalt believe in thine heart that God hath raised him from the dead, thou shalt be saved.

— **American Standard Romans 10:9**

> because if thou shalt confess with thy mouth Jesus as Lord, and shalt believe in thy heart that God raised him from the dead, thou shalt be saved:

— **New International Romans 10:9**

> That if you confess with your mouth, "Jesus is Lord," and believe in your heart that God raised him from the dead, you will be saved.

— **Revised Standard Romans 10:9**

> because, if you confess with your lips that Jesus is Lord and believe in your heart that God raised him from the dead, you will be saved.

— Simple English Romans 10:9

> If you confess with your mouth that ``Jesus is Lord" and if you believe in your heart that God raised Jesus from death, you will be saved.

John 5:24

— King James John 5:24

> Verily, verily, I say unto you, He that heareth my Word, and believeth on him that sent me, hath everlasting life, and shall not come into condemnation; but is passed from death unto life.

— American Standard John 5:24

> Verily, verily, I say unto you, He that heareth my Word, and believeth him that sent me, hath eternal life, and cometh not into judgment, but hath passed out of death into life.

— New International John 5:24

> "I tell you the truth, whoever hears my Word and believes him who sent me has eternal life and will not be condemned; he has crossed over from death to life.

— Revised Standard John 5:24

> Truly, truly, I say to you, he who hears my Word and believes him who sent me, has eternal life; he does not come into judgment, but has passed from death to life.

— Simple English John 5:24

> I am telling you the truth: The person who listens to my teaching and believes in the One who sent me has eternal life. That person is not under condemnation. Instead, he has passed from death over to life.

I John 5:13

— King James 1 John 5:13

> These things have I written unto you that believe on the name of the Son of God; that ye may know that ye have eternal life, and that ye may believe on the name of the Son of God.

— American Standard 1 John 5:13

> These things have I written unto you, that ye may know that ye have eternal life, even unto you that believe on the name of the Son of God.

— New International 1 John 5:13

> I write these things to you who believe in the name of the Son of
> God so that you may know that you have eternal life.

— Revised Standard 1 John 5:13

> I write this to you who believe in the name of the Son of God, that
> you may know that you have eternal life.

— Simple English 1 John 5:13

> I wrote these things to you people who believe in the authority of
> the Son of God. I wanted you to know that you have eternal life
> now.

John 20:31

— King James John 20:31

> But these are written, that ye might believe that Jesus is the Christ,
> the Son of God; and that believing ye might have life through his
> name.

— American Standard John 20:31

> but these are written, that ye may believe that Jesus is the Christ, the
> Son of God; and that believing ye may have life in his name.

— New International John 20:31

> But these are written that you may believe that Jesus is the Christ,
> the Son of God, and that by believing you may have life in his name.

— Revised Standard John 20:31

> but these are written that you may believe that Jesus is the Christ,
> the Son of God, and that believing you may have life in his name.

— Simple English John 20:31

> These proofs have been written, so that you, the reader, might
> believe this: Jesus is the Messiah, the Son of God. If you believe this,
> you will have life by his name.

Witnessing Made Simple
Order Form

Postal orders: William J. Cooper, Jr.
                 1132 Lake Point Dr.
                 Westerville, OH 43082

Telephone orders: 614-899-7372

E-mail: wjcooper@aol.com

Please send **Witnessing Made Simple** to:

Name: _____

Address: _____

City: _____ State: _____

Zip: _____

Telephone: (_____) _____

Book Price: $13.99

Shipping: $3.00 for each book to cover shipping and handling within
            US, Canada, and Mexico. International orders add $6.00 for
            each book

Or order from:

ACW Press
5501 N. 7th. Ave. #502
Phoenix, AZ 85013

(800) 931-BOOK

or contact your local bookstore